Free Verse Editions

Edited by Jon Thompson

Current

Lisa Fishman

Parlor Press
Anderson, South Carolina
www.parlorpress.com

Parlor Press LLC, Anderson, South Carolina

Printed in the United States of America
S A N: 2 5 4 - 8 8 7 9

Library of Congress Cataloging-in-Publication Data

Fishman, Lisa, 1966-
Current / Lisa Fishman.
     p. cm. -- (Free verse editions)
  ISBN 978-1-60235-200-1 (pbk. : alk. paper) -- ISBN 978-1-60235-
201-8 (adobe ebk.)
  I. Title.
  PS3556.I814572C87 2011
  811'.54--dc22
                                        2011001728

Cover design by David Blakesley.
Cover image: *Green Engineering Object*, David Mabb. Oil on
Honeysuckle Fabric, 42" x 63". © 2001 by David Mabb, with
thanks for the artist's permission.

Printed on acid-free paper.

Parlor Press, LLC is an independent publisher of scholarly and
trade titles in print and multimedia formats. This book is available
in paper and Adobe eBook formats from Parlor Press on the World
Wide Web at http://www.parlorpress.com or through online and
brick-and-mortar bookstores. For submission information or to
find out about Parlor Press publications, write to Parlor Press,
3015 Brackenberry Drive, Anderson, South Carolina, 29621, or
e-mail editor@parlorpress.com.

Contents

Acknowledgments

The section called "Lining" was published as a chapbook by Boxwood Editions (Chicago, 2009); thanks to Joshua Marie Wilkinson and Lily Brown. Portions of it first appeared in *The Laurel Review* (Maryville, MO) and *Mary* magazine (Moraga, CA).

Portions of the section "Questions about snakes" have been published in *Columbia Poetry Review* (Chicago) and *Upstairs at Duroc* (Paris).

"The Holy Spirit does not deal in synonimes" was published as a chapbook by Parcel Press (Denver, 2007) and a portion of the work first appeared in *Parcel* magazine; I thank Andrea Rexilius. Thanks also to Andrew Kadel and Seth Kasten, directors, respectively, of the Burke Library at Union Theological Seminary in New York City, who invited me to study Barrett Browning's Bibles and transcribe her marginalia in 1997-98 and again in 2007. It was helpful to present a scholarly paper on this material at the "Author as Reader" Conference at University of Salzburg, 2003.

Portions of the section "All winter couldn't fit outside a book" have been published in *Talisman* (Jersey City) and *Sawbuck* (online). The first poem in that section ("Being *in* common has nothing to do . . .") is made of notes by Kaoru Yamamoto from her lecture on Joseph Conrad at Vaxjö University, Sweden, 2008. The poems beginning, "Only Acts & Is" and "But another one said" contain material from Vincent Van Gogh's *Letters*.

Current

Lining

vibration of the wind

vibration of a current

a curtain of the leaves. Decidedly,

      vibration. Lust

rust, moth consume.

Stay then as a cloth

      door   waterfall   piston

all the moons are apricots

has the message a vibration

the mobile has, clanking in the wind,
five blue glass birds
against each other

*

The bamboo screen divides the room
being written to you again
in a very bad time apart from us

so it doesn't want not to go on, this meaning
given

If she likes
a melon, can you have a
haircut in the kitchen?
the white chair folds up and there were days
I didn't see you for years

was missing

Cautiously
the child steps around the yellow
caution tape, says

"I'm cautious."
        Words or
do so, will you, on my neck
the thing you spoke of, wrote the neighbor

Here's her grass green
sheaf of paper and the sky
unlining it; flew
in blue and opened by
my author self / other self
I'll show her
how to cook

What do you remember learning about democracy?
It doesn't seem to matter if you can't recall.
In this way the inside and outside were brought together,
as Jupiter the largest kept hold of its numerous moons
and many smaller bodies
pressed on the Earth.

throw CAUTION
to the wind

Don't get attached to THINGS

my mothers said   (echoes)
over the plants

Love all the ones you're with
and the ones you can't be with too
Then you have a MUSIC ROOM

My apartment is quiet I live alone
under the volcano—Mrs. Lowry
is my name and both the forms
are cisterns

Sound it out around my ear
as Sandra says: honey or
money
        tend her
in pencil or type her
a letter

The child wants a kettle too,
says whistle in
the fish
        Oh are stirring
up vibrations, starring up the drum sky
        bowl turned over
were you under the bow &
number
of strings to a theory, a fiddling
hurry
        child says sleep
in a cello bed

In being explained the music of the spheres
I understood the stars make sound, moving

A reason came to me
in the knelt-down light of the streetlamp night

My bus went by
water and earth in the child-air
and my ear received a little

outside
        Have you been
in the small sound?

One and one were finding there
it hard to speech, to catch
in the mouth the slip
past all that may be said, may not   I mend in you
a portion thereof, there fire of

                        a lit self

leaf (*to* leaf), a need
for water, not
to flee

the continuing comes around and around the not said
                                        to seed it

Flown, what did flow out or fly,
can go to love the sun she

spoke of color in a yellow skirt,
split light through it

There was RETAIL
        &
     OFFICE
     SPACE

the sky hadn't ordered yet

If it were possible to read the books
being gathered in a shoebox on the desk—

but those were shells in the shoebox
The books are stacked on the desk

In a hurry, the wind has a hole in it

      NEW
      VIEW
      REALTY

just going by

The palmist saw a tree line
where the head line ought to be.

Well there can be houses
built in trees and trees growing out of the ear.
The head, like cabbage, can be made of leaves.

Clothes don't matter anymore.
Where was that voice
to come from—

oh! it went back in

the scaffolding from eye to breath,
an apple in the worm
we made a wound in to investigate the wound.

She said to me "our mothers
being happy in the 70's"—

the sentence kept afloat.

A lot of police on the platform today

    DRAW A GUITAR
      AVOCADO
    A NEW PLACE

A letter is composed of the parts of the many bodies of angels, if
I misprision an ancient belief like the inner or outer point at which
another shape becomes possible, as that which occurs can be that
which has not, but may.

I admire the daylilies because they are tall
and maternal, like men

the archer & fish are twinned?

Small-armed, J says the cake will be sweet,
"as sweet as seaweed,"
lifting the cat to the window

Photographs don't reach a conclusion, someone suggested

Must continue seeing the street the bus drives by
as being somewhere in the many
people crossing, had a camera with a flashcube

Of primary importance, it is still
the weather occurring around you

A camellia got sketched on the notebook cover
(I meant, a camel) and 〜〜 for water

under a ⚬ and ☾. Intentions passed in swimming

out past the buoys
return like this
smudge on the lens

Waves love the traffic going by
out of the corners of their mind

Who called it starry, night
and where
to think the pattern planet-like and clear

So full of harm has come the civil speech

One can't live in one's time and love, but does
and asks, because it's true ("the rain is drinking the flowers?")
unless it isn't, anymore, a private
dilemma
       A winter
can be blank sublime

and the mint to crush
representative: one hand here

the rest, cloud
cover over the mountain
Vision
can be said to fail

Because the water carries voices
differently across the water,
has anyone intended that?
Or the white moth in the sunlight where the parsley grows.

Immense activity of flies and bees.

The ocean can be green or black or
gray or blue but can the ocean be a white moth
on the planet in the garden or one that flew
very much in the pleasure of good company
born and has died several times since.

We stepped into the sunlight I was walking toward.

The many times one looks across the fire at the opposite
and he was some people we wanted to know, to keep recording
what was said at four: what time is it? a red thing
unlike power, more a message you could carry in your mouth.

The room is far too bright for me to see you in
and, also, you are not here.

Has there been circling for thousands of years
or (let them sing) has something stopped.

In a concordance all the words
are all the words, and otherwise I had a feeling—caught there.

Open your arms to leave things out
and if we hear it, reversed.

It was of the fire but not in the fire, the world
becoming-visible, as it was

already here, you and
nothing I can find to say, nothing *about*

you are going for a walk? or a phone rings
at the water's edge; it's broken

out of the law, no going back except eternally
we do go back --- shore? flame? ground? electric

of the air? & coming forth you do appear
to meet me in recurrence, there was breath

to cast upon the waters, there was breath to animate the clay,
much else has not been known or touched or found

I hope you are home when I call

Questions about snakes

A pencil can be sharpened down infinitely—
having learned this, a person says, or we
might know better than to choose the number seven.

Placed here, in the contents of your mind
a wooden spool exclusively
for making ribbon. It's childish

and intricate, the nets lain down,
the strewn road.

The pages waved, made wavy by the damp
imaginary   Have you been

writing of peas have you added
on the wheel? Friends become loved
become lit become surfacing

guitars, even Ann
home from the wars.

Little funnel blue path through the clouds
that curve around another cloud
is just a description for the ones I love.

Infinity of pattern on the stones
are circles, lines, the future, past, the secret
present on the shore.

A man who shook the olives to the center of the net
had left his glove. It shows up in the photo
and a dream includes a face
with no connection to what came before.

Sometimes the name is wrong,
the wrong beloved
way to read. Bedecked with stars

the night flies out.
          Particular numbers
of letters get written in colors.

Sheets will be hung on the twine.

Soul, betwinned, extending,
of each given thing.

The boy did tell where the stars fell,
pero, Cassandro, he was not believed.

The horizon makes itself a path
when the trees that frame your view of it
outline a funneling down to the sea.

Having failed at journeying once again,
the donkey hauls sandbags to the ristorante.

I am not learning Italian in order to read Dante
I am not reading anyone
except to speak of the missing

> Ballot box,
> Ballet Pox, "keep it simple stupid"
> makes a nice war.

Once in the shadow of a great mistake,
the plots all tangle into failure
except "the bright obvious stands motionless in cold"
from which there was no spinning off into an own.

A sea is a glass
mare, la mer, sea.
The waves break over and break
off: a central note, C, comes apart.

Questions about snakes were you dreaming

the night-flecked grass and the snake

under the line, under the sheets hung on the line

Were you in the grass barefoot in the night between

one tree

said nothing

heard

A cloud fell down

on the roof of the barn

Was it very many

days like that

Volcano made 2 boys

pour vinegar over baking soda

every time it was summer and when it was other

flew away

Here yellow mouse

I have a black hat

and the hoop was gold, being pushed with a stick by a girl

through a sunfield on the eyelids in a moving train

Oh my dress

is not my dress

I like your song

I am stung

by a yellow jacket in the Chevrolet

and wish you were

my one true love

I have a friend

the Tilt-a-Whirl

in Orfordville, said Bobby Ross

at the beauty shop—he has three hands

for braiding hair in seven strands; will take two months

to sculpt a ship on someone's head

Here 11

kinds of kale

have insect lace around the edges

The darkest green becomes you

house in the forest, cat on the counter

There were a few sentences but they did not cross

your mind at the base of your spine

They floated by

the bus you carried to the airport

& walked away, carrying only

your face in their hands

It had been gently removed

At the start of summer

dark comes from the ground and wettens

the air so socks don't dry where they fell from the line

in the general lack of clarity about the sun's force

at the end of the day

There are a few sentences waiting around

the path from garden to house in a small town entirely

lit up by the glowing rear-ends of fireflies, and in the category

of that which illuminates number also desire, the anti-shadow

falling simply across

Very loud wind in the poplars—here is the sound being sent to you.
Whatever's contained in a letter you come out of, come read
a way goes through. Nor are the trees on fire could you say.
Coming in to see how they look through a window, you send what's
contained to you. The poplar leaves shimmer like bells in a way.
Whatever was found on fire could you not say: go through.
I am reading this to you.

Very clear sense of the unfinished only beginning. Requiring you to
keep the letters moving and away. As close as possible. The trees,
though poplars, are separate from the people lying underneath them
in the shape of bells, were two or any people ever in that shape,
a sounding shape, the wind blew. Could reading be contained.
Do you like this fire ever coming out of what was found, a person
in a letter in a way. Whatever you say, do not arrive. It's hard to
hear. "How come" we say for "why" and yes the darkness very dear.

The reason sleep is important to poetry is that you need more
darkness in your head.

Don't matter none, the window guy said, the screendoor just now
clanging—unclear who—a summer sound.

It was true that early nightfall was a feeling or texture of what
was heard—mothers calling in their kids—and that separateness,
between the calling and what was felt, could be about to happen:
an expectancy attendant on some distance or split in consciousness
(vibration).

If we lived in Italy, the child would stay up as late as anyone and
end the day by being out in it. The mothers would be free to
walk off the front stoop or back steps. Though nothing particular
happened, the sensation remained, or recurred.

Believing that these impressions had to do with each other,
I looked up the Nurse's Song with its contracting last line,
And all the hills ecchoed. In the rain the notebook becomes a letter,
out of the blue.

Others get written in a small house for chickens—a coop—adorned
with circus poster, silk fabric, stolen desk.

Conversations wander around and sometimes meet up in the
seeing.

Sit down with me, a person said, yet I can't speak of small things falling from trees.

Then turn and walk to where the not-grapes hang on the vines and the shapes between.

(Last night the child said we can hear not-thunder and see not-lightning and first he said the moon is beautiful.)

In Spring we were sleeping toward a density which would act as fate came in the rain to sail a marvelous time into flowers. You should know this, you bee staggering out of a peony.

I mean I remember the red sheets as much an impression and feeling as a color, though I remember that too. Frogs in the marsh have a happiness she believed on the stoop of her cabin that periodically flooded. All those sounds have a difference at night, where we might go.

As for the congruity of dreams, a week apart, the fireflies lead the last light up the hill in the direction of the orchard, the woods, the next field over.

Down the hall from the child's room, I think about what to say to the inside of my head. This is the problem ("angels tall as apple trees"): not-hearing fills the notebook with traffic (north-south), birds in hickories, birds in maples, birds in black walnut, birds in sick birch. Just before going upstairs, the child demands "to read" a particular cookbook from the top of the fridge.

Wishing for sentences to float through and disappear, this too.

Not really

quiet enough

the owl in the hula-hoop looks fine

without my glasses, now I have them

Inside the mechanical dolphin

were woodwinds for the queen

It's summer so you know

a place for making, do you now

fill all the jars with pickles and all the jars with jam

and all volcano molds with vinegar & soda

on the table for a person turning six

In the long museum hallway they have moved

the suits of armor—now a monkey offers honey to the Buddha

in a single glass display case   Just to mention

sex creates the places, not a person

outside a place, in time

Along the edges of the table lay the flowers

set by outlaws in the greenwood, though the woman wanted fish

& got it, "silver burden" in a net—it's something I am reading

with a person only five, not a Pisces, but he peers at

the small ink illustrations of the table

with the flowers on the edge

In the lunar house it will be obvious

which trees have spherical leaves, why it is hard

to pinpoint the faraway olive, the near birch

Set it down
across four strings—this giant
field across the way
is part of her approach

The mother cat came carrying
one kitten at a time, from barn to barn to house, five times
until the country grew
four walls around her and a roof

Sure animals
have bodies that are good to watch
stretch out, I'm trying to
fall down on skis although it's summer and the friends are
picking Sun Golds for a market—what was fire, might be
fireblight, the pears

Poor Grace, who climbed the ladder,
pail of feed in hand to fill the bin back up
after the door had not closed on the chute
& all the grain came spilling out, and she was 8 months out to here
said Serafina in the story in the kitchen

Snow's coming soon is not the truth
but helps to sell tomatoes in mid-August; it's a pitch
the 5-year-old invented on a Wednesday

Some minutes of a change between the sounds
the one stone balanced on another

"Donkey, are you sad about your body?"

The mountain working out its name, *Victoire,*
could be like telling Cathy things across a table.
Things are rock and mountain-side.
Sky, horizon, scrub.

Stone and stone and stone and stone.

Tiny oak leaves we collected made a man glued to a pinecone.
The face James painted on it happy, like the donkey
he collected from the trash, its half-deflated body in his arms
half-flopping down the street. Henry patched the donkey with a stick
so now it can be sat on, even bounced around the kitchen
on the cracked, star-patterned tile floor.

Of snail-shells littering the mountain-side it's strange.

The iron bedframe standing in the grass
creates a bed of grass, a frame around the grass
illusion toward the traveled-toward.

"A stretch, and you are in the heart of things"

Sally Jean, the Bicycle Queen
will come on Wednesday to the fair, good argument
for property / against / because / to see you there

that the body had strengthened over time and made a conduit
for what to flow through, that to flow through, thought to flow through
one letter at a time, one friend who hates money, one car in the blue
field

age-of-reason-like, abandoned heap
outside the maze—*then I do this to make it do that*—
then we found the telescope (the time is going up)
beside the sentence where we found more time
above five, below six
especially ragweed growing out the windows of the field

The grownups are hoeing *around* the onions, Andy said to Taralee

Insects are in sections, noticed Aristotle
A worm came out of the table made of apple wood, wrote Thoreau

Too much grass in my eye to see well—there go the lanterns
you can take apart

Relation of part to whole makes the in-sect body and its name

Dear *Freund*
don't know about the Sandman or the miniature drummer
but is a "round chisel" really a "gouge"

These are pears, said Augustine, that were not mine
nor the ribbon Rousseau's

Our dog Pearl
ate the flesh off a pig's skull
in the whitening sun

You were saying, knives and grass?
A tree was felled at a slight angle
(held at one end by its own branches), and the hewer walked first up
                                                    and down . . .
The same axe was used for both scoring and hewing!
This process seems difficult but it was fast.

Also, there is E. W. asking of stars, some open shirts
at the market, speaking of bones, and the radish man's
vegetable form of the rose

There is a color but not that color

guitar and the glass
slide

We were saying SING IT! but not really

putting the sounds in as they change

bird call—traffic—airplane—wind in poplars—wind in maple—
car turning in—18-wheeler driving past—wind in hickory—door
slamming—screendoor opening—screendoor flapping—
water running—everything else—the same, repeating

Which things lead toward / lean toward / leaf toward / fail toward

the garbage pick-up ROAR

bird's nest in pear tree

(first we saw 3 eggs, then beaks & heads . . .)

very few hours in which to write
nothing, of necessity

coming back to a feeling in the rooftop where you couldn't hear

the rustling exactly

And this is sexual the roof of the mouth
is not the mouth

nor the name Aloe Vera a person's

but the doubles keep appearing in the bean rows
where also the BEANS will be

about this high   and curved

depending on the scale

this, this, this

is a thistle

in English, a needle not so

much a need, or solely that

to sew into

graph paper, body

by which what's known is

tabled: set it,

the table / tablet / rasa

per amica

(by the light of) the crinkling

sound of the birds this

being what I hear one moment

veering off

Fastening

the wind to the shape of the wind

the wind to the turn of the wind

the corn grows in corners, in squares

the roads too

In a fell swoop the school came down

the mind at fault, the bricks

could be pictured there

Had been looking around in the time

around the time, may want to say chime

or the name of the cat's Tom Horne In the Chanterelles,

the fluted mushrooms, nothing known

to be that orange

Often in love

with two or more guests in attendance,

the field has a particular, imaginary charge

my dear

The foxtail by the road resembles foxes' tails specifically but briefly

in a light also fox-colored, didn't mean

to write it down

Steep angles come to mind, if you were asking

that question. Has darkened, the day

into the moment

the train goes by. Didn't answer

I didn't answer

could be following down to the sternum

the silence turning in one

Modigliani's portraits of women

are really the mother, we noticed at 8 and 4

Holly and Lisa

how do you like this

being seen by the paintings she was in

But no appearance

of intended words ("had leafed so often")

through the books

Had leaved, have left, it felt

familiar not to ever

call on them

Through circles in the curtain in the morning

shade to shadow, jester to guest—sun sorts

the tall brides and the small grooms

James and Fin found 102

acorns to feed the pigs, or for making soup

James washed his socks in a pot

with white cakey pieces of soap all summer

by the side of the house—the little pot

with no cover

It's blue

"The Holy Spirit does not deal in synonimes"

40

Note

I transcribed the following material from the margins of Elizabeth Barrett Browning's Greek and Hebrew Bibles at Burke Library, Union Theological Seminary, in New York City in 1997 and 1998 at the invitation of then-director Andrew Kadel; I was assisted further in 2007 by Director Seth Kasten. With spacing, page layout and, in two extreme cases, typography, I've attempted to replicate the visual character of her notes, although hers are spread across many more pages. All underlining is her own, as are all quotation marks, with which she often includes the name of the source. I have not added any text to that which I transcribed.

Where Barrett Browning wrote words in Greek or Hebrew within a phrase or sentence of her own, I have brackets. Because I don't read Greek or Hebrew (although I copied all of those words down in my notebooks originally), her translations, phrases, sentences, arguments, exclamations, questions and comparisons existed, for me, long after their occasion had fallen away—that is, the words that provided the occasion for her words, her "synonimes," were in a way absent. In that curious condition of reading, what was compelling were the textures and tones of her thinking, heightened by the apparent fact that her primary concerns were accuracy and pattern: accuracy of translation (for the sake, importantly, of accuracy of figure) and continuity of figurative patterns. Sometimes she records an aesthetic response or an association with a literary text. Often, in the spirit of discovery or dismay, she notes the inadequacy of her King James Bible of 1611 (to which she often refers as "E. V.," for English version).

The following translation by a kind of material reproduction is limited in other ways, of course, since Barrett Browning's tiny cursive in faded-to-brown ink, sometimes pencil, can't be seen here, nor all of her excisions of her own notes and comments— emphatic swirling loops, sometimes chains of x's, over portions of her marginalia. And all of the text transcribed here constitutes only a small portion of Barrett Browning's marginalia in her Greek and Hebrew Bibles.

42

bitterness of mind.

to look on

to hear

to join

to intwine

    a coin on which the fig. of a lamb
    or sheep was imprinted. Compare.

    to forget

Parkhurst is of the opinion that
the Hebrew wd does not signify
interpreter but interceptor
        mediator, the offices appointed
                        as advocate.

Parkhurst objects to the idea of divination and translates it thus—
        surely teach accurately.

and one shall grope in darkness

Those whose eyes are open.
Closer to the sense than the
English version, "the wise."

no material tabernacle can be
intended or implied by this word.

applied to silence of voice as well as
to quietness of situation. Compare
Dante's "dove 'l sol tace—: &
Milton's "The sun to me is Dark, and
                                silent."

The word is applied to silence of
voice, as well as to quietness of
situation.

Dante says Dove 'l sol tace— and
Samson Agonistes, or rather Milton,
under his name, The sun to me is
Dark, And silent.

rather in [   ], the name of a place than
in the jawbone.

like nothing: good for nothing.

with whips, with goads attached to them like the stings of a serpent.

    a rock. [   ] a vibration of light.

who built oceans of sepulchral
mansions for themselves

      <u>a word came to me secretly</u>
<u>& mine ear received a whisper of it</u>.

There is a resemblance tho' no
<u>coentity</u> between this to the [   ].

the incarnate

Can the fire be the separating fire of
                          Death.

48

We are said to be baptised in it; and in other places we are said to be
    baptised into the Dead.

                        fully opened.

Dr. Clarke considers this expression to mean <u>fulness of grace</u>, after
I think Dr. Pierce who quotes from Euripides

The <u>church</u>. [   ] The Lamb's <u>wife</u>.
    not exactly acc. to the Septuagint
    but very <u>nearly</u>.

                    inspirited?

The division not equal: but <u>as</u> <u>each</u> <u>had</u> <u>need</u>.

written in the yr. 58-- 4 or 5 yrs after
the Edict of the Emporer Claudius by
which all the Jews were banished from
Rome

justitia   Hebraism   <u>justificatis</u>

justificatio

circumcision arising out of this faith &
uncircumcision remaining this faith

justificatio

> The Jews should glorify God for
> his truth. The Gentiles for his
> mercy— The fellowship of the
> Gentiles & Jews justified.

"One thing we may remark, that there
is no mention of Peter, who, according
to the Roman & papistical catalogue
of bishops, must have been at Rome at
this time!" —Dr. A. Clarke

comparing scripture with scripture

> I think he is not right. Is it not,
> rather, that [   ] means the spiritual
> things? which are [   ], the
> internal impulses of the Spirit?

in the mind   <u>in the word</u>   in the action

"since ye ought to come out of the
world."

That is a clear precept. I do not enforce it now.

if in anything ye be <u>variously</u> <u>minded</u>.

walk by the same rate.

justice   <u>a</u> church   <u>a</u> house   <u>a</u> church

    <u>a</u> pillar   in yleih   in spirit

The latter is grouped especially to the
<u>believer</u>, the <u>brother</u>, & the sister.

The Holy Spirit does not deal in synonimes.

of <u>self</u>-interpretation: not any
prophecy of Scripture is its own
interpreter—written reference to its
context. <u>Horsley</u>.

May it not conversely refer to the voice from Heaven making prophecy, intimating that without the Spirit who did appear in a Dove's form while the logos was being uttered we understand not what we do?

The Heavens were of old, & the earth being formed (or constituted) <u>out of</u> water & <u>by means of water</u>. We have here the <u>precise</u> <u>doctrine</u> of the Wernerian school. Werner not only taught that the earth was brought to its present form by the agency of water, but also that it was primarily made in the water, & afterwards emerged from it.

See Parkhurst's version of these words. "Even (as) the sparrow findeth her house and the dove her nest where she has laid her young" (so shd I find)

to fill with food. The crib where he is
fed.
       applicable figures.

to watch, hasten the almond tree
flowering <u>early</u>.

Hebraism concerning the <u>living word</u>.

1/ the primoeval subsistence of the
truth.

2/ the testimony of it

3/ The experience of it in the spirit
soul & body   in the flesh

as the calm sea can not look toward
the sun

But ye are <u>washed</u>, but ye are <u>justified</u>,
but ye are <u>sanctified</u>

the spirit crying 'Abba'

Then the crucified was the [   ] of
Hades – the place of separate spirits:
of death – the place of corrupting
bodies.

A vision of immortality

rrumpet in this too.

Naphtali is a spreading oak, producing beautiful branches.

compare to the preceding verse.
Surely the same word shd. not be so
very differently translated, as it is in
both the Sept. & EV

Instead of [   ] propose dividing the
word & connecting the second part
with the succeeding clause!

The stars can be numbered but the depths of His understanding are
numberless.

The Hebrew [   ] is yet more emphatic. The English v. not at all so.

stones, grave

Tho' He can number the stars, the depths of his understanding are
without number. The repetition is preserved in the Septuagint,— but
not in the English version.

Angel in the English version

the animal man.
the intellectual man.
At least so it appears to me.

unto the rock

Heb. To dwell for a time – as a
stranger

See the first Psalm. The connection
between this 29th + 30th verse, is
beautiful.

And what is the remedy for this non-
forgiveness of the [   ] or [   ]?

Go into the rock. I cannot doubt about
the meaning of the passage: and it
seems to me very beautiful.

to wish with the eyes in order to see more distinctly

the Dawn

Does not this mean their faces shall be
opposed to the flames; that the flames of
God's wrath shall be reflected upon them? Of
the English translation, "their faces shall be as
flames" I can see neither the construction nor
the meaning.

not merely a scroll, but a written
scroll. & written by the finger of God.

He will reduce it to the original
chaotic state —when the earth was
[   ]. And the very means by which
order & substance are ordinarily
produced, the [   ] and the stone, shall
produce confusion + hollowness.

        the transitory world.

I have hurried thro' my life like a shuttle.

        islands – wrong

not filthy rags; Parkhurst says a
garment of ornaments, a shewy
garment – shewy in the light of men,
but polluted – a garment of
testimonies – in allusion to the law.
I prefer the former sense.

"in a horn / of fatness" says the Sept.
In a place of strong light

The light acts upon oil as a constituent
                              in vegetables.

And its light is darkened by its clouds.

        From [   ] To fall in drops.

        in its reflections

P. says "In Persia, to this day, their ink
which resembles our printers' ink tho' not
so thick, serves them not only for writing
but for the impression of their seals."
Comp. Rev. VII–3, 4.

Can this mean "on account of the
Word the glory of thy name."?

The moon being of a changing glory
—sometimes burning, sometimes
obscured. P.

What a mere whispering is heard of
Him—and the thunder of his power who
can understand. The E.V. does not give
the strong sense.

That the earth may turn—
The influence of light on the
appearance of the earth. Perhaps –
Didst thou know when thou shouldst
be born, or whether the multitude of
days shd be great – See Dr. Wilson's
                              grammar.

And Rachel said, With great
wrestlings have I wrestled with my
sister, and I have prevailed: and she
called his name Naphtali.

              to "<u>intwine</u>"

Aquila is plainer than even the
septuagent and is closer to the sense
than the English translation.

The Septuagint is nearer the sense
than the English version is.

              "wrestlings of God"

                    feel, touch
          to feel through, rummage through

              grope   let some one touch, feel

God hath entinwed me and I am entwined, and I am rendered able.

that he rent his clothes, and said, Alas,
my daughter! thou hast brought me
very low, for thou art one of them
that trouble me: for I have opened my
mouth unto the Lord, and I cannot go
back. very forcible and <u>beautiful</u>

Is it not rather <u>think</u> than speak?
Speak, ye that ride on white asses

Why should our translation say
"grasshoppers." <u>Locusts</u> is the word; &
the figure is incomplete without it.

Does it not mean simply, he
sympathized with them? The
expression is strong—His soul panted
with <u>their</u> labor.

<u>Secret</u>

"His name shall be called <u>wonderful</u>."

wonderful. See Isaiah. The English
version translates it <u>secret</u>, and yet
in the very next verse where the
same root occurs, it says "the angel
did wondrously." The Septuagint is
correct in this verse tho' not in the
very next verse

This is singular. Compare.

And the angel said unto him, Why
askest thus after my name, seeing it
secret?

a word came to me secretly, & mine ear
received a whisper of it. Heb.

Now a thing was secretly brought to me,
and mine ear received a little thereof.

little = whisper

The Heb. wd is [   ] whisper

beneath the opening of the eyelids of
the morn? Lycidas.

Can it be the snares of the soul—
the Septuagint seems to second this
reading- Yet the E.V. says "the giving
up of the ghost"

In thoughts from the visions of the
night, when deep sleep hath fallen
upon men, Fear came upon me, and
trembling, which made all my bones
to shake.

<u>In maddening thoughts</u>

<u>my maddening</u> thoughts

The English, "Therefore do my
thoughts cause me to answer,"
is not sufficient.

All winter couldn't fit outside a book

By turns you may be someone else, you may

imagine I have cooked a pheasant or a hen, and eaten all

the feathers in the book   or made a law

against it: self

the pivot of the shoulders of the bird is turned

The many centers of a circle

can impede the walk around, or standing still

you saw you there, both poised, both frayed.

I found a ship too

in line 7 anywhere & carried it forward until I appeared

until it appeared combined

Being *in* common has nothing to do

but being-with-one-another

with and *with*

Better so.

and for a time he came out of himself

being is "*outside itself*" an exteriority

it cannot relate to *itself,*

This relation   the place

and the position of the ship

and the beginning of ours

It appeared to us that the side of the house was more smooth than
glass and more slippery than ice.

and there in a body, someone else's.

It is with that absence—its uncanny presence, always under the
prior threat of a disappearance—friendship is brought into play and
lost at each moment

One thinks to provoke another into thought, then the hands

Could all that

window, in the winter, being held inside a sleep

be brought around the fence the dream erects

or something said about the day

In the middle of 4 lines, the mother's face

alive and is

not dreamed, an armload full of roots

A spark flew further than the fire

crossed the eye, unburnt

The mind could veer, as it would like

to be seen too

against another's pressing back

the real

& all the sun are shadowing

the plants and animals continuing

things semi-

startled or to start

inside the mouth

Henry, James, Brian, Richard, Glen and I
are trellising tomatoes—kinds are listed
in a notebook (Henry) and a poem (Brian);
had been planted in the Spring by Henry,
Jonny, Sarah, Mary, James, me.

David T. gives furniture
approximately once a year—first the pink settee
& satin cylindrical pillow, then the sparkly blue chair.
It all goes in a dollhouse that we rescued from the sidewalk—
picked it up by its gabled roof and walked away.

The notebooks have been disappearing
& there are things I want in them. Do you remember
the dolphin-torn, the gong-tormented

March 19

The sea is different when it goes through each

(nymphs quired $\longrightarrow$ torn

$\downarrow$

paper

unmended

where the notes are

A – C – B

And *were* the golden apples of the sun! in interlocking figure 8's
across the page of questions for the queen's two bodies and the cat's
appearing as a shadow in the garden, could we say it once occurred
and having once occurred, continued so and so and so and so,
various & manifold in ways to be made out among the rustles and
                                                        the whirs.

An adequate shape in which to play the sun, the mother thought,
stretching out her arms to do so though the child thought she was a
                                                        nightmare
in the impromptu game of charades, had yet to be found: like this,
                                                        the child said,
his fingers spreading out: for *sun* just use your hands. A vast
amount of basil grows adjacent to the gravity box—
grain flows down from the sides, toward the center, through.

And not the silver apples of the moon have any basis in the surface
of the lake at night, and not the clothing scattered on the rocks
but in the myth of symmetry & opposition; in relation to a given
could we still say really has a shadow any bearing on the body in
the garden, as a queenly double of that aspect of the garden that is
lushest in the shadow after all? & manifold & various the rustles
and the whirs, not having, occurred.

The snow came from the sky

and the sky was made of snow

according to Daniel, who has a blue car

and a red car

for interpreting the sky

How dark it's beginning

to be early in the meantime

No one is asleep

or lovesick anymore

Some women on a bridge were from a story:

a green bird

on a garden wall

akin to a crease in the present

war in the world without end

In the beautiful

paper sky

a pauper's clothes

drift by. The boat should stay

stark white, she says

but hears, "unfinished, unreal."

She says it's more than what you think—

the clouds and grass are fine,

the water too, the boat as is.

If you paint the brightness of those birds as they fly

not everything can be entwined, misspelled or spilled.

The banker put a z

in Liza my name

for a minute

now the current

only Acts & Is, in existing beings or Men

For the lake is almost gray today & laundry hangs
from window to window on opposite walls

There are others
by which if one works in too dark a room
the work usually becomes too light

so that when one brings it into the light, all the shadows are too weak.

I find the book open to the very page you were thinking of
when certain obstacles appeared, and I heard this with some wonder

that you really asked Ezekiel what made him go naked and barefoot
three yrs

that you asked in all seriousness, "why he eat dung, & lay so long
on his right & left side?" the desire of raising others into a
perception of the infinite, was the answer reported

Could I be talking to anyone—definitely not
at the same time yes

just as xylophone can start with Z and example with X
in a poem of the alphabet signed zozo I love you

It must be imagined why

Level planes or strips of different color, getting narrower and narrower
as they approach the horizon, were recorded by the painter

But it seems to have turned out differently in the end
In the evenings such a sadness, including a round moss-roofed house

Must there have been people in it, could there be
among us some there still and besides
there is a place I wish you might see

First of all I intend to visit that place one of these days.

But another one said: Mind you, to see it like that
one must not look at the local color by itself
but in conjunction with the color of the sky!

And that one said: But it is the local color of a green field
or a ruddy brown heath, which leads one astray

Write soon, V wrote his brother
who did write from the office, to complain
there are not enough pictures

And how does it sound, the air of summer
at the end of summer, waking up to hear "winter sun,"
sensation of

is there somewhere I'm supposed to BE?
The men are pressing cider in the driveway
Child says to violin, are you going to DISAPPEAR?

Often I wish for a letter or phone call made
in the infernal method, melting apparent surfaces away
displaying the infinite which was hid

so there is someone to write to
In the distance, wrote the painter, I see a very curious drawbridge

Might be
the gate of the plums
the time of the plums
in a green book with color plates
Ah my dear angrie Librarian
the page is very soft—a building has a coat
the doves fly out of
That book on gardens being older than the land
was made in England about Japan
My Brian, says my James, drives a car
while standing on his head
The cow in the meantime fell off

The edge of the world, one of a few, that you were eating in
kept going around like a mass of moths around the world—
the edge & center can separate; concentric circles can move

Might be
grass birds
grass brides
you thought you read that week in the cabin when the pigs were shot
Grass bides, you changed it to, so what, there are some things
on a twig some mold & eggs I bet that can't be seen, buds in Spring
                                        which always should
be capital, like Winter and Fall though summer can be small
The heat comes on December third, bending the peculiar
pink paperback Charles will know
the one I mean and the words I stole

In the course of any shadow thought the harmony of spheres
the "they" is very open, could be we
who opened up the book of all the feet
and matched each to a body,
those with hooves
or toes or paws, many varied
kinds of claws, innumerable birds

Outside the book the V's head south,
V's of birds, in general birds
might be
as air to water not at all
the opposite of fish

As in a portrait face with asymmetric features
here and there, the nose off-center, eyes askew
I caught the branch the parent and was born—well flocks of snow
start falling on the weather now
The page is very cold, flying out the bus doors when they open, plural they
might be open
might be shut

Meanwhile the face in the orchard in the sun
can shine at once or crookedly through leaves as part of one.

About the Author

Lisa Fishman lives in Orfordville and Madison, Wisconsin and teaches at Columbia College, Chicago. She is the author of three earlier collections of poetry: *The Happiness Experiment* (Ahsahta Press, 2007); *Dear, Read* (Ahsahta, 2002); *The Deep Heart's Core Is a Suitcase* (New Issues Press, 1996) and most recently the chapbook, *at the same time as scattering* (Albion Books, 2010). In Orfordville, she lives on a farm and orchard she and her husband, Henry Morren, started in 1998; in Madison, they live with the poet Richard Meier near the Yahara River. She has a six-year-old son, James Fishman-Morren.

Photograph of Lisa Fishman by Elizabeth Park. Used by permission

Free Verse Editions

Edited by Jon Thompson

13 ways of happily by Emily Carr
A Map of Faring by Peter Riley
An Unchanging Blue: Selected Poems 1962-1975 by Rolf Dieter
  Brinkmann, translated by Mark Terrill
Between the Twilight and the Sky by Jennie Neighbors
Blood Orbits by Ger Killeen
Child in the Road by Cindy Savett
Current by Lisa Fishman
Divination Machine by F. Daniel Rzicznek
Physis by Nicolas Pesque, translated by Cole Swensen
Poems from above the Hill & Selected Work by Ashur Etwebi,
  translated by Brenda Hillman and Diallah Haidar
Puppet Wardrobe by Daniel Tiffany
Quarry by Carolyn Guinzio
remanence by Boyer Rickel
Signs Following by Ger Killeen
The Flying House by Dawn-Michelle Baude
The Prison Poems by Miguel Hernández, translated by Michael
  Smith
The Wash by Adam Clay
These Beautiful Limits by Thomas Lisk
Under the Quick by Molly Bendall
Verge by Morgan Lucas Schuldt
What Stillness Illuminated by Yermiyahu Ahron Taub
Winter Journey [Viaggio d'inverno] by Attilio Bertolucci, trans-
  lated by Nicholas Benson